(1)
Gayle's secret Life.
The Art of health

Introduction

On a warm sunny day, I was born, July 27th 1968, the weather was hot and the Beatles

Were around. Kennedy was just President. It was a time for joy and peace. My mom had 10 albums of me alone since I was the first born, 1 out of 3 children. Although my sister was only a year and half younger than me and bro was 3 and half years younger. I was the only summer baby so I like the heat the most. I was a jealous baby that I was told. My sister came home from the hospital and when I found out she was staying permanently my love for her went out the door. The attention that I had was gone. I felt lonely and alone even at that age. In my early childhood stages; every time my father came home it was like a t.v. show; we ran to him and said

daddy, daddy; until one day he came home and told
us to call him by his first name, Leland. It wasn't the
most easiest name but it was tolerable and cool
calling a parent by their first name. Eventually Lennon died
probably and Kennedy was shot so the hope was
doomed. My mom told me a story years later that I
could have been a still born or even worse lose a limb
from her taking medication that was not prescribed.
She was often a woman that ran on impulse without
thinking except she was a stay at home person. I did
not think she would harm me but intentionally she
did at least mentally. She did not get her period and
the doctor told her the rabbit test and blood or urine
test all came back negative. Then she felt a miracle at
7 months. That was me. To make matters worse she
did not have to wait until her water broke. She kept it
a secret so that she can avoid going to doctors. Years
late I go into strange men's cars without thinking
twice. Sometimes even guns to my head by where I

hooked up with the wrong people having jobs at a strip club. But not your ordinary club. The Harmony theatre on Church Street was the sleazy of the sleaziest. It was a lap dance place and girls constantly getting arrested by touching below the belt. My friend was visiting, and the language we used was "waitress" meaning that we got tips so we worked as a waitress if anyone asked. The tips were the same since the men liked new meat and ignored us after a while; unless your were really hot and then had regulars. Every hour or so we had to dance on stage. I was stage fright and not too comfortable with my body but it was either that or forfeiting 10 dollars in exchange for not doing it. I was frugal and wanted to look good so my pride ate me and put on a show. I am lucky to be alive but the bad memories of rapes, assault and laughter always linger within me and trying to keep my head up high. I still have some nightmares what I have been through. I wanted to write a book of memoirs to commiserate the passing of my father, the dad that I never knew, and the struggles I had as a woman, health related problems and family issues. I wanted to help others and teach people that there can still be goals and aspirations. Time can heal all wounds; weather 1 year or 50 years. Everyone is different. Some take longer.

Keeping the weight off was a struggle for me. But staying away from twinkies and

Cupcakes, dingdongs , whatchamacallits (chocolate bars), mounds, almond joy and

Snowballs were just the beginning. Never mind hersheys. I ate that for breakfast,

Lunch and dinner. My mother and dad were mentally

ill. My mom had bipolar disorder.

My dad was schizophrenic (later died from

complications that were not known because

Of his illness unable to communicate) believing it was cancer related. He never liked Medications because of his side effects. He wrote on millions of spiral note pads. His hand writing was worse than a medical doctor. It was columns that looked like this~~~ ~ ~ ~ ~~~~~~ ~   ~~ ~200 ```~ ~ ~. Later in life before he was gone, he was writing a book that never was published on math or accounting. He was delusional, but some part of me really wished he did. He twirled his hair often, mumbled, and had bulging eyes that scared anyone. His birthday was near Halloween October 30th. But he did do my math homework and took me to doctors when I stepped on a wooden stick in the park. There

were some, not many good memories. My mother
was diagnosed later when my father died to get
disability checks which are not too much but better
than welfare, about 200 dollars more and don't have
to deal with those badgering workers for a pay check.
If your disabled; you are usually to ill to go down to
the office and get hassled and one is State, one is
Federal. I learned later filing taxes on the welfare
system is indeed possible. There were agencies that
people volunteered to help get benefits.
I grew up with two siblings. I am the oldest and most
prone to witness things that the others were unaware
of ; when the police came nearly everyday, when we
got robbed

From the painters, when my father was in episodes and we had to run for our lives down the emergency staircase. At 5 years old seeing all this was unbelievable and see it ; I could not express it in words. I was withdrawn in school, quiet, showed off my assets(ass an vagina) to get attention. That's what I learned from my mom when she wanted money or material things from men. I also did little school work until I woke up from my funk and became debunked. It was difficult to concentrate and was suffering with depression. I started school at this time when my father lost it, he was never the same after that. I chose to write since age 5 because that's when my

memories set in; before that pictures

(2)

were like the Brady bunch. He was an

accountant, middle class, and went from a Mr.

Rogers look to Jerry Garcia/orthodox man. He

once dropped me at an affair in a catering hall ; I was

around 5 and used the bathroom. Took a piece of

cake. Next thing I knew ; I was on the floor with

people looking down on me. I wasn't as physically

hurt, but emotionally suffering and shocked. He also

spilled milk on my sister at age 5 "spilled milk

syndrome- I will give you something to cry about"

He chanted; he chanted a lot. Not too many of it

made sense to me. But I guess it did to him. The one

good thing he did was my homework. I even got he

extra credit questions right. He was a math genius.

But he did it in a way that was so I couldn't learn

myself. He did not have the patience to explain

it so he just did it. I had to go over it myself; and

not too much knowledge. It was very

frustrating. I always fantasized for "normal

parents." This was the same person who I

trusted, and held me in the past as baby. My

mom used the broom, and covered my face for

protection. To this day, I don't like my face

touched too much. (unless makeup to cover imperfections). Later on I became a lap dancer, go go dancer, and then finally a nudist posing for artists. I always liked art since it was a form of escape from my negative and toxic environment. Some people like dancing ,venting out in t.v. It was relaxing and soothing for me and seemed somewhat normal to the daily effects of horror that I had each day. When the cops came; it seemed so routine, that I asked my mom, where are our friends, and why do you have black tears? (mascara). As she was chasing him down the stare way with mace in his face. I smelled because of the bed wetting , and the kids

teased me when I got there

Grandma did try to help. At 5yrs. Old I was in

the neighborhood McDonalds and asked her,

"grandma who learned this is French fries?" 'Its

not tatoes, their fries"!; after the 3rd time that she

reiterated that "Gayle eat your potatoes." Yum

the comfort food being with granny and

enjoying a Sunday out was thrilling enough at

that age. It was nice to be with her. I have some

fond memories because being the oldest; She

spent more time with me.

We were waiting for grandpa, when he showed up; she said he got lost. I said, "no he is right here." My aunt always new I was entertaining, after the circus at Ringly Brothers, I put on a big act with the animals, and I was the host, my whole family was rolling on the floor laughing. It did give me some self esteem, but that came and went many times.

My schooling was always important to me since my I missed all of kindergarten. The teacher grabbed my legs as I was holding on to my mom and was swinging me with her. It was not fun at the time. I could not cope. The next year, I was so withdrawn my teacher had to grab my hair to participate with the other children.   Later on I would suffer from anorexia and social anxiety. I read it ran in families. My dad was diagnosed with schizophrenia when I was 5 yrs old and just started school. I was used to a middle class life with cars and play dates when my whole world crashed on me before my 6th birthday. My mom was later diagnosed with bipolar disorder in order to get benefits when my dad died of cancer in my 30s. I felt a relief she was diagnosed and that he died. My pain was going and never gone, my thoughts were positive but

still suffered. story in mom dropped out to go to

the familiar beauty school. The same greese which

we watched over and over. My mom came into

money a few times. My dad was on Candid

camera, her mom sold the house on Crawford

ave. in coneyisland and back money from social

security that my dad had. Her illness made her

spend thousands within a summer. She treated

her friend out the one that introduced her to the

college degree nutty professor , and her kids,

and we got a paint job since we could not longer

see the white walls, just say we Picassoed it

up,and then some, added some curse words.   I

went to 4 different high schools because once you left one, apparently they didn't take me back. Brooklyn, JHS, Ditmas, FDR, Bais Ezra,crown hts, and John Dewey, Don't forget summer school . Welcome Back Kotter; New Utrecht H.S. I was going through a spirituality phase and went to a girl yeshiva. Bais Rivkah , the Rabbi's daughters went there. My aunt influence me to go, I was the head of the school with the cool kids. What a turn around. Then my friends moved. That's when I wanted to go back to public school. My aunt took me to a cruise vacation the graduating year. Actually I was in summer school making up a class, not college classes for remedial work. But I thought positive and passed! I was really surprised all that I have been through, but never the less, I was happy. I did not know that was more in store for me. That was a real accomplishment. My dad did help me with math homework, The way he did it, he solved the problems and I reviewed it . The system did work, but then I realized I did not really know too much. My aunt who has a masters told me just show up, the school usually repeats it yearly and you get credit writing your name and just being present. That did work, and have the diploma and other certificates to prove it. My aunt was good in away taking me places as a child and young adult, but to her everyday was a party, smoked too, and did not have a set schedule or a job that I really needed. The first time I took a puff I was 10 thanks to her. I also moved out at that age. My mom calls it running away my grandmother calls it visiting my dad where he lived at Peekskill with her. I called it trying to be free. The court system was blind and had to return to my abused place. I of course rebelled by not listening and crying all the time, but I coped with it in my own way by partying, listening to music and staying up late nights watching television. There was one that I particularly remember; prisoner cell block age a time of the bad girls club in the 80s. I felt real grown up watching x rated shows. My mom was just happy that she won the case against my grandma since she always called children services on her and I always complained that I was hungry. They just said that she was a good mother. Good enough to let me stay there.

A few years later when that part of the family moved to Florida they sent us a 2 fare trip by Amtrak because we did not like to fly on the time. A lot of fighting with my siblings. Florida in Tampa was great, Bush Gardens, Disney , and lots of friendly Buffets. The fight broke out with my aunt and grandmother when it came up that she told me not too eat so much so I would not be as obese as my aunt. My aunt kicked her ass along with my dad because of the extreme abuse they suffered where food was scarce. She used it as an excuse for growing up in the depression and that's why she always bought Tupperware whenever she was at a hotel or other social event. When she moved to nyc with the kids. My boy cousin who I adored was in a car accident and lost his leg by amputation. My female got cousin got raped by a security guard both were between 5 and 8 yrs. Old. I was close to both of them, the boy had a crush on me and anyone in a skirt. I jokily asked my aunt to marry him so the money stayed in the family, she agreed but serious. That is one of the many times that I put my foot in the mouth. I couldn't go through with it no matter how tempting it was. I rather be homeless than be with someone that I am not attracted in that way to have a sexual relationship. That decision was a good one. They both won a civil law suit. Together for millions of dollars; eventually moving to Kentucky, the green state and peaceful state. Cheaper and less environmental disasters. I enjoyed going there. The beds were huge and the view out the window was grass, cows eating and children playing. Pools, friendly folks, and cheerful birds chirping. I felt like a princess and friends that came to visit were kings. I did everything from babysitter to lap dancer. Off the book jobs suited me with my flexible schedule since I loved art and travel so much. I began liking my body more and lost some weight and exercised to keep up with my families heart and cancer problems. I went from one extreme to the other.

I knew that I would not be a doctor so I took up

acupuncture, Reikki and massage, and did have

a few clients. Posing nude or giving a massage

at someone's house was still a chance to take. I

am petite. Some of the men were twice my size

and weight, you always get exceptions that were

nice and not too much pressure. I looked

forward to those. I never got the fast food jobs

that my peers got. I did yearn for them., The

smell of French fries was tastey to my

imagination. Upon graduation, I went to Mandl

medical assistant, Nurses Aide school, and

certificate for home health aide. Eventually I did work enough with mentally challenged enough to get medicare and SSD. I did wind up finishing college. My mom was a high school drop out so I did not want to be with her and my dad was an Accountant from good Ole Brooklyn college. I was never sure if he had a CPA or masters, but then I learned his mom, my grandmother helped him type his thesis for graduate school, and years later he aimed for the CPA but never completed it. I felt sometimes they made an odd couple, but they had chemistry, yes sex! Dr. Ruth was my inspiration. I was only frightened when I walked into their room and saw his penis; it looked like a snake. People did not know if he became schizo from the pressure from school, his job, kids, drugs (LSD) , his mom from being to political or frugal, or my mom always pressuring him to give her more and more and more to his three children who he adored. I do believe were were all wanted, but we were not dolls or babies forever. That is what they both wanted. To be passive and stay small with little or no needs until reality set in. Then our clothes change, we met boys, placing more demands to go out more. They both did not know what was in store. We used the wall as a canvas and expressed art. It was fun and let us vent our anger and frustrations as children. My mom was in another world sometimes and was worried from paycheck to paycheck to survive. It was scary and almost homeless, crying going to the welfare agencies; coloring books there. My mom had a crush on Gabe Kaplan, and my teacher looked like him at that error, Mr. Keller. I have a great picture of him. My mom put on a good act, and went to every school trip that year. Including the hostess factory! That was the time I thought she cared.

I like painting and art. I escaped through art and being part of art. In the future I did some nude modeling to get used to my body image and love myself again. It was difficult to look deep within and struggled plenty but I did it. My father's sister gave me 2 compliments about my art and how pretty I was; otherwise , she used to beat the s---t out

(3)

of me and say how stupid I was. There were plenty of times that I cried myself to sleep and wished I was somewhere else. The one book that

I did enjoy reading was the Diary of Anne Frank at the time. I can relate to her by being her age. Her struggling and trying to stay strong many teens can identify with this. She was also a late bloomer and petite. She spent her most precious years in insanity and had to make the best possible ways to cope. Her fantasies, her crushes and having support with her family gave her a bright way of looking forward. Although she might have had a slice of bread and some water, she knew tomorrow would be better. People compare Hunger and AIDS to those times. And the government pays the holocaust survivors and the welfare and SSI pays the others. Also the War in the Middle East. Coming back mentally or physically disable will have repercussions. They get reparations. That is a little something to cover some damage done. But her and my dad did my math home work because I was struggling with my psychological turmoil. I always liked older men; I never knew why; until I took up some classes. I was psychology major and even before studying Freud. I did date older men to replace my father image that I had . I had fantasies of a "normal life." When a man or woman took care of me. I liked the nurture instinct. It made feel good and comfortable with my environment. I was in the womb again; feeling safe and secure. Two tragedies that developed through my childhood and young adult period. My cousin lost his leg from an amputation and I got struck by AIDS. It was unbearable especially after growing up with both parents suffering from mental illness. I was in a steep depression and had anxiety issues. I was in a rut and hard to get out of it. Fortunately there were support groups and my sister. She is really my savior besides my grandmother when she was alive. She grew up in the depression era

and saved food. She was frugal, but later , I felt
like I was in the dirty dancing movie with the
late Patrick Swazey. We went to the Concord
and Pines Hotel. She took the morning muffins
and lasted a month. It was delicious. I never
leave home without Tupperware. It's a
necessity. When I was younger , I cared what
people thought taking refreshments, then I
didn't care. The hour dourves were tasty
anytime of the day. During my visits to the
Concord hotel, pines and trips on cruises with
my aunt or grandmother, I slept around. I just
melted if someone said I was pretty, I didn't

have to be a Freud expert to know that I was
missing my father or needed attention. Yes, I did
get a std, hpv. It was not curable but was under
control. I became a health advocate and you cant
get it from casual contact or if you use a condom
while in a relationship, that was safe. The stds
were overwhelming, I didn't know how many
forms of hepatitis there are , but D was one of
them . I became a political advocate like my
grandmother who died right before my father.
She often talked about the Rosenberg's and
Women's rights. She became a feminist and read

Feminists magazines all the time and Ms.

Magazine.

Becoming more Jewish and the rituals besides

being a penny pincher, led me to OCD

(Obsessive Compulsive Disorder). I am not

thrilled of the "D" but coping with that part.

I did see psychologists, psychiatrists and social

workers about this. Most of the time, I

diagnosed myself and was my own doctor.

(4)

 I was often misdiagnosed with anxiety and

bipolar. As it turns out, I did research myself and

had histrionic personality disorder with some
DID (disassociation). I did not want to
believe it at first, but the more I read it, and it
said that if you have 3 out of the ten symptoms,
its YOU. I had all of them. I knew that I can
help myself. Every new year, I discovered other
treatments to improve my self at least for the
time being. A fresh year, and a new me. My ptsd
(post traumatic stess disorder) was somewhat
under control.

I constantly struggled with body image and
eating habits; I hypnotized myself in not eating
junk food because how sick that I got in the past

eating twinkies and donuts all the time. I know the names of chocolate bars by heart. The roaches became out pets since the monthly exterminator didn't do a good job, and our dolls resembled celebrities from soap operas. We played with both of them. It bothered me when the bugs fell on my head from the ceiling and the kids made fun of me from smelling. But I learned to ignore them at an early age so that there would be peace. I saw too many school fights. Eventually the folks and plates were unusable and insects always came out at night. I preferred going to the grocery store and getting plastic until the Muslim owner molested me. I

Gravitated to the candy. They were all my

friends and had a personality of their own. Some

were famous ones that I made up. The ding dong

was sexy dark chocolate. Twinkies commercials

and t.v. said they live for years. The recent

family guy took a trip looking for twinkies at a

play they were movies because they never die;

and the sarah silverman show had an episode on

that too. I was in another world when I watched

comedy central.

But I did let go all the pain and turned my pain

into power. I let the demons that drew me to

this comfort; finding another way to fulfill my void, a happier and more silent way. Yoga, art and meditation to name the few. I was in recovery for drugs, sex, and food addictions. Even "normal" people have addictions working to much and over exercising.

Celebrity paparazzi was also a hobby. It came naturally since my mother snapped photos of me all the time and she taught be my artistic talent when she drew in coloring books by tracing the outline with a dark color and coloring in the subject with a lighter color. Those small instruments gave me some ideas and inveterately used this as an idea and a muse. I was more outgoing when I got older and more uninhibited when it seemed appropriate and not in dangerous situations. There were times that I did get into strange cars and get "candy" from weird men that I did not know; fortunately only luck I can

(5)

blame for being alive in this crazy world. If John Lennon can be killed by a random nut; Craigslist killers are on the loose in the 2000 decade. That was a difficult time for me. Pursuing a job as a massage therapist and an art model; I frequent these websites often. Mostly people are legitimate. But if you can not trust your own parents; who can you rely on. I know nude sells and being comfortable with my body as an artist and an art model was important to me. I had to be involved with many "wackos" who wanted sex instead of the art of painting, photos or film. There is a fine line to them with porno and art. I have my limits and had friends die of AIDS or just die by ignorance. I would try to scout them out over the phone. Many times it is unpredictable but my intuition and street smarts sure did help in my predicaments. There were close calls where I know that I was in danger with a weapon or some verbal discrepancies, touching me inappropriately and lying to me.   I know this is a dangerous occupation especially going in solo. I usually do

bring a companion, sometimes they cannot make it. People have day jobs. An artist had a completely different schedule; more flexible but changes day to day. I just had to fend for myself. Everyday I hear of another girl or woman die or raped, usually in Long Island or NJ by the water. At this point. I was in recovery from drugs, sex, and stealing, lies. What else can happen. I was also in the psyche ward in my 20s for just taking

time out and in my 30s jail for 2 days for
hopping the trains. The psychiatric ward was
misery. I committed myself for the weekend and
full evaluation. I didn't think that I would get
out. The nurses aide gave me a massage, and I
was in the geriatric ward. That's what they had
available. I had a toilet in my room with a
skeleton on it with the words Hazardous I felt I
should be worried what they would give me. I
was the one with mono and hpv. They were not
very friendly and the staff didn't drive me home
from upstate like they promised. I felt relieved to
be home with my cat and fish. Although they

didn't last long because of my housing situation.

It was dark ,un kept, and smelled. . The jail was

just like the movies , one toilet for 20 women to

share, rodents and female security guards that

felt you up. It was not the Hilton. But we did

fantasize about getting out. Some were doing

hard time and being transferred from the holding

cell to Rikers Island. I prayed that it was not me

because they gave me a song and dance that they

did not know what my previous record was . I

know I did not do anything but take a pair of

panties at Kmart or a piece of chewing gum at

the local candy store. That was 10 years ago, but

is still on record. When my friend Dave cam to

bail me out . He is an attorney so he could testify

that I am really a good person. He was not he

most reliable but the most respected person I

knew. I was so happy to get out the next day,

and hoped my cell mates would understand.

There are no clerks and I had a disability pass. I

had to get from point A to B. I felt desperate not

to be late so I can achieve my accomplishments

but it was a catch 22 in order to get out of the

house I had to make sure everything was in

place so I thought that I would have a good day.

My OCD was catching up with me. But the

books say that if you can live your life day to day which barely that I did, then it was not considered a big problem, but it was getting there. I did try therapy far and in between. I took breaks to go to school on psychology and art classes. Focusing on hoarding and meditation were important to me so that I can combat this issue. But I learned that I had a void to handle, and it took time to recover. It was and still is an ongoing struggle but I do have support and group that I attend. It is ever lasting. There is hope out there if you need it. Fortunately these concerns are becoming more recognized nationally and internationally. More trained therapists are taking into consideration that people do not need to suffer and get educated on this matter so we can help or reduce the target that is really bothering the patient. This will take time since there is no right answer. Everyone is an individual with unique cases. The first group that I did attend in therapy I was 10 when I "ran away" I met my grandmother in the pizza store when I was supposed to be at school and my mom did not feel like taking me that day. I hated the groups. I did not think I belonged there and she did. My mom used to pick me up for lunch.

One day I came home went to the bathroom and she commented for a little girl big things come out of me. Her language skills was not the greatest. Once my sister pushed my brother and hit his head on the tv while she was picking me up for 15 minutes. I spelled stitches and mailed it to my grandmother . I was 6 years old. At least I did not have foster parents that hurt me. She used to say people burn and kill there kids. She came close. I also sat in Kings county and Bellevue Hospital and sometimes I even shared at group or family meetings. I liked meeting new people even then and had a niche for this field. I hoped one day that I can help people too; it was a struggle going to school since I missed half the time. One time jimmy carter sent pictures to the children that were home for chicken pox. I don't know where that picture was. Amy Carter was my age so I adored the time he was in office. I was always a democrat. The groups went well and it helped me realize that I can be worse off. The groups varied from day to day. I sometimes went to art groups, dream interpretations circles, music groups, and spirituality groups and each were in different places. The people were all different and many personalities. It is not a one size fits all when it comes to these sessions. The facilitator and co-facilitator that were led by professionals and other times by peers. It can be beneficial if the person has or had similar experiences with the empathy if they can identify or relate to the feelings of us. I did feel comfortable when the I was heard and really listened too . I used to hate when I came in the next week or next day and the psychologist or social worker did not remember what I told him or her and even some of the receptionists did not even remember my name. This can leave a bad taste in someone's mouth and discourage them from coming back. I also liked when I got to bring my significant other or sister to the sessions. Sometimes their insurance did not cover them or they just felt funny seeking professional help for themselves and this was the easiest route to go by. I did learn a lot with my sister. We were to co-dependent on one another and we got off by being the "mother" or guardian" in the relationship. I was older even a year and half, and she was less "wild" than myself and had better judgment. But she was judgmental which caused friction. This takes time and I know what we were doing but was not fully aware. This did help us. My partner and I are like the odd couple. I save he throws out. We try to compromise and not get so angry that it is painful when I feel he is disrespecting my stuff. He is trying to help the situation and not hurting me. At the time I have a difficult time thinking that way; but I do try and it takes time. One step at a time like any other negative habit or addiction. Individual counseling, group sessions, and couples treatments are all so different with positives and negative in all of them. Fortunately outweighed by the positive. One issue that was pressing me was when my grandmother was

alive she promised me her Ford car. It would

have been my first , but she was angry when I

disappeared to Israel since she like Russia the

communist country better. I did not tell her

because it was in the summer, Yavnha Olami

meaning a jewish name for come friends, I was

one of the oldest who attended. It was

inexpensive and once in a life time. I am glad

that I went. I did not want my sister taking

responsibility for moving the car back and forth

on alternate parking. I did learn when someone

gives you something ; do not hesitate and take it

immediately. It was a learning experience. I did have future opportunities to take something pronto rather than wait. The saying get it while you can is true. I did overcome this and got valuable information from not giving in to the things or people that you want. Another burning thing was when my mom hit me so much that I was black and blue all over , I was barely recognizable. She denied doing this so much and said she went through the actions similar to what my father did. That was bull shit and lies. She just did not want to face she did this or get in trouble by going to jail or the psyche ward. If she did go anywhere I was not going to back her up. If you did the crime, you do the time. She was disturbed by ignoring the situation of what she did and the effects that it had on all of us. My brother and sister have both emotional traumas. Because I was the oldest , I remember more aspects and hit me harder. I did have difficulty in sleeping, eating disorder (too much or nothing at all) and withdrawl symptoms. My mood swings made my coping skills more manageable with having friends and other family members of whom were always there when I needed to talk to someone. My cousin in

Kentucky and in Florida on occasions did visit
quite frequently and although she was going
through some of her own personal stresses, she
was always there for me. Some of the night
clubs that we went too were convenient in the
90s; palladium, lime light, café iguana, Shout,
Chevy's, TJ Bentley's bar, Wheelers in
Brooklyn and Nell's. I did not always have to
have a drink to feel high. My bipolar was
enough. I was too frugal (cheap did not sound
good) to get a drink, I felt great when men
bought it for me. It showed me someone cared to
make me really happy and concerned that I was

happy. My favorites were colorful ones like blue whales, grasshoppers, bloody Mary, woo woos, and Pina coladas, apricot sour and other sour beverages. I felt like if it had apricot in it or coconut, it had to be healthy. Just like if it was a granola bar or had nuts in the ingredients, it was a great choice. Later on I did go to physical therapy, it was a gym for the poor or the elderly. I learned by nutritional counseling I was consuming too much calories and not enough protein. When I was a child, my mom stuck a bottle in my mouth every time that I cried and my sister was always thinner. She was born 8 pounds and I was born 7pounds but she had food allergies so she recovered and was a picky eater. I used to take advantage of that, and often steel her food when she was not looking. I did one of those things, I pointed and she looked, when I did grab the food on her plate. I did not think twice. There was also a time when I did smack her or take a roller skate and whack her one . I gave her a permanent tattoo with a pencil which I do regret to this day. It is small but I recognize it. I showed my love in odd ways. In this case sticks and stones did break my bones. I was so angry being called hippo or fatso that I wanted them to feel the pain also. When we drew on the white walls, we did make a mess by writing stuff on the walls like profanity; fatso, hippo roach back for my sisters huge birthmark ,and being my brother was the only boy. He got balls or dickhead. He used to light fires and hurt animals for his aggression. We did have 2 poodles for a short time. That's when I felt there was some normalcy. One my father lost walking , the other my mom sold for some money. There was always tough times. I grew up thinking scratches and bruises were how it were supposed to be. Then I had friends who were like t.v. sitcoms and then I fantasized that I was in their family, and started wanting a good life. I was also intrigued by other parents of how close they were. They were genuinely concerned for their children's best interest and wanted them to succeed. They save up for colleges. They did not even want them to work so they can have their energies for studying or just being a child. They had focus on what they wanted to help them fill their endeavors. These kids did do well. They went on to college and graduate school. The one's like me were homeless, in shelters or foster care. I was always

sad when my aunt or grandmother left. I was in
hysterical moments. I wanted to be with them.
They had the side that I always wanted and
dreamed of . I knew if I was a good girl maybe
this will one day happen. I went through phases
being spiritual and attended classes on g-d or the
higher power. They explained do not say g-d in
vain or event write the name so the hyphen is the
acceptance of that. I also did not preach about
this, I felt like it came within since I hooked up
with plenty predators or child molesters
claiming to be religious. Hypocritical
testimonies turned me off. I was more for the

righteous aspect, and the belief that practice

what you say is true. I am not perfect, but do

contain myself in the right circumstances. This

guided me to realize that there is hope and

sustained a compassionate heart. It guided me

though very tough times in my life . I did see a

rainbow on the other side of the dark path. I did

get the help that I needed through this journey.

It was a long and winding road. It is never

lasting. I cried myself to sleep plenty a night,

but did pray my own way. When I was not

expecting it, misfortune did turn to wealth, and

not necessarily money , but the things that I

wanted and cherished were in reach for me. The void was being filled. At times to be honest, I did not always feel it, but did affirmations, and wrote things down what my goal were and are, and felt someone or something was listening. The Buddhist and my spiritual fate along with my Jewish culture all wrapped into one. I also had similar friends that went along with my feelings so when I felt sad or blue, they were only a phone call away. I influenced other family members or friends, and they seemed also more at peace. The John Lennon era always gave me fond memories and some part of me thought that I could have be reincarnated from the 1960s. That is where my true heart and belongings were. The time for true happiness and peace. Everything seemed surreal and not materialistic hand outs were a need. Family and friends were of importance. Joyous and love were enlightened by this uncanny way of just being. I knew my society was a long way from this and the cynical feelings most people have were there and the aspirations were lost or even gone. I never have up hope.

Some of mentors were there in the process. I seek most of them out when I was in my dark days. People think that it just falls on your lap without making any effort. That is not true. The effort is tiresome and exhausting; it pays off at the end when you're assertive. Passiveness and aggression does not get you anywhere. I learned this when trying to get what I was going for. Getting what I want sounds selfish, my needs were a necessity. There is a fine line, In order to help others and be in the social work or case managing positions, self-care and relaxation methods are good to fine tune and have the resources to accomplish this. Burn out is fast and easy. This can be eliminate with stress diminishing. Everyone is stressed, how to handle them is different. Imagine on the train and there is a bad day with your family, please do some relaxation methods so nobody else gets hurt on the train or even worse at the job or at school. Many problems can arise from this. Someone can get hurt or dead with projecting ones anger on another person that the punishment is not fit for the crime. Just ignoring them or thinking good thoughts is better karma without actually physically touching or harming them or the individual.

I still have thoughts of my mom touching herself

when I am right there and she had her

headphones on, and hitting me with the

broomstick when we were not perfect angels.

She also got pregnant by a Pakistani man when

she was by Coney island

visiting her family.   I was not there at the time,

I was staying by my aunt but I did hear bits and

peaces that I could have half Indian brother or

sister. The first time it was a miscarriage, second

time the IUD messed up her insides. She was

depressed for a while but I could not really see a

big difference in her chronic mood swings she always had.

I coped with my irritability with support groups and attending NAMI metro. I eventually got a job with them doing IOOV (In Our Own Voice) presentations to know that there is hope and that I am not alone. The NAMI stands for National Alliance of Mental Illness. There is a colossal of us around and being that it is well known, there is less stigma and I volunteer at the GMHC. They changed the name so the acronyms do not appear in the name ; just the initials. The security guards in both places asks for ID . Some people feel threatened by the confidentiality, but I do not mind it. I feel they are doing safety measures and it will protect us to a point. The activities and networking that I gain from these meetings outweigh the negative. I feel more safe and secure. I also enjoy that we are not alone. Dr. Sarton Weinraub was a young psychologist and he did not really guide me enough, but I did gain support that I needed by the person centered approach. He taught me that we living in the moment and being here is better than the past and dwelling on my misfortune. Friends and family are important. Dr. Paul

Greene guided me through meditation, and Dr. Weiner was an ass. He was so into himself. Sometimes I wonder if they get their licenses from a Cracker Jack Box. I feel that if you really want to go into the helping profession ; be genuine and passionate that really want to help someone in need , not be judgmental and always have references for the person who is in trouble. These different approaches vary when the counselor listens and does not talk or the counselor does talk and barely listens. Some have a mixture which is the most positive way of dealing with the client. When they do not take my health insurance or most insurances, then they are mostly out for themselves. They are narcissistic themselves. Someone once told me that most counselors or psychiatrists have issues themselves. It takes one to know one. They are also in treatment therapy. You do not have to be "crazy" to seek treatment. Support and understanding so we can go on with our lives. I started seeing a therapy in grade school when I "ran" away to go to my grandmother. It was court ordered and I was not ready for that. But I went with an open mind. I was a big 10 years old and realized that I was open to new things even then. I lost the trial , since then the judge twisted my thoughts and asked loudly "do you want to go home" your mom can go to jail for a very, very long time! I thought it was forever. It was almost as emotionally painful as when my father lifted me up and dropped me in the air when I wanted to touch the cake in catering hall. In my mind then I thought he said yes when I asked. A child's perception is very different than a grownup. Not to mention I did lose the case; and granted summer rights and vacation time; but I know I was in a desperate situation back with the enemy and torture. I could not bear this and cried myself to sleep on a nightly basis. When I came home some similar circumstances happen. I used my fire escape as a balcony. The child welfare came when my grandmother called. When I asked to eat from stress; I looked so hungry and the worker might o f thought that I was starving . My mom always gave me a dirty look for stating that I wanted to eat all the time they were over. They invaded our privacy by opening the refrigerator each time. They must of came three times. I barely bathed and went to school because it was too cold to do both. The landlord did not provide any heat and became a truant but managed to not

get left back. I went on the minimal basis. My

only sibling that did was my sister. She couldn't

catch up; later found out she had congenital eye

problems that corrected with glasses that she

hardy wore. But surgery was out of the question

since it was barely there. My mom used to hit

us with a broom stick and cover my face and

eyes; and my dad threw things like milk or juice.

The mace and raid were on hand by my mom

when we ran down the stairs still smelling from

bet wetting the night before. The super was still

alive; and helped call 911. Later she died of a

stroke or heart conditions. The aggravation we put her through I am sure did not help. I used to go clubbing when I got older and one of the bathroom attendees in shout resembled the super. I told my sister and she agreed. Every time she gave me a paper towel; I had a flash back. I went clubbing ,drugs and sex. Not necessarily in that order. I wanted to escape reality ; I lost my Ids at sometime by not knowing where anything was; vomited and got a STD. so I hope nobody follows this example. The rock bottom I had was more than one ; and learned to love or like myself better with self-help book, support groups, and yes being and artist and posing NUDE for them. I read it can be empowering and change how I feel about my body. In the beginning I was shy but took a minute to evolve. I got used to the beauty of being alive in the moment and appreciating the human body.

Eventually I tried every school in NYC and variety of photographers that were looking for models from petite, fat, skinny athletic, and average sizes. I knew you do not have to me a super model. I was not to crazy with the waif look or the mannequin type anyway. I met many sculptures as well and learned many mediums of interpreting the same person in a classroom setting. I can look different from everybody's work. Some were abstract; others were based on realism. I enjoyed how it captured the genuine gesture of the pose. It reminded me when my father went naked in parkside park for attention; and got arrested. Some nightmares still linger on. But the difference is I get some help from My friends. I joined support groups such as NAMI, GMHC, and VOW, National association of mental Illness, Gay mens health crisis, and Voices of Women Organizing Project. Each have a uniqueness of their own, but share a common way of contributing and giving back to the community and individuals. I was lost and in the mist of finding myself. These organizations guided me down the right path. I was abusive to me and violent with others. I threw things, had temper outbursts, and threatened suicide for attention. It is unexplainable of the type of help and encouragement that I got to take one day at a time and treasure each moment as though its the last. I still struggle from time to time , but now I can handle the rage better, and seek help without being embarrassed to call someone or my life support. In AA there is a sponsor; in real life, a mentor is needed for situations that can not be handled at a borderline moment. Finding peace and serenity can be achievable, and justice can be made through this networking. I am capable of anything, I am beautiful, I am unique. These are affirmations that is of my own and identified as an ownership that nobody can take a way; along with breathing properly; deep breathing, and eating healthier. The mind and body connection is important awareness through difficult times.

The gmhc offered support to women with cancer or AIDs, the voices of women helped women have a voice to speak of abuse that can be physical, emotional ,social that people ignore until its too late. Nami has trainings to cope with mental health and the benefits are overwhelming. There is always a answering service with a empathetic person on the other line. You feel that you are never alone. Beside these offers on a daily basis; I am involved in yearly walks for breast cancer, mental health, cancer, and AIDS. Giving back to the community and sharing with others while others do not have a voice or can not make it because

of illness. That Is a big accomplishment.

Some tributes were photographers and artists

that I did TFP (trade for print) Vladimer Kenner,

Barbara Hanson, Tanyth Berkley, Zefrey

Throwell and Michael Berkowitz.